Honey, I

But...

I Love You More!

Dear_____,

Personal message: _____
_____
_____
_____
_____
_____

_____

From:_____

HONEY, I LOVE GOLF, BUT...

I LOVE YOU MORE!

What She Needs to Know If You Want to Keep Teeing It Up

JODI WALKER

RIDGEVIEW PRESS
Valencia, California

Published in 2010 by Ridgeview Press, Valencia, California

Cover design by Kimb Manson
Copyediting and book layout by Claudia Volkman,
Creative Editorial Solutions

ISBN: 978-0-9719443-3-6

PRINTED IN THE UNITED STATES OF AMERICA

For information regarding special discounts for bulk ordering or non-
profit organizations or to inquire about arranging a speaking event,
contact staff@HoneyILoveGolf.com.

**This book is dedicated to my family
for their love and support.**

To my husband and my daughter, who have been patient
with my ever-changing projects, I love you.

Mom, I know you are smiling down from heaven
and cheering me on as always. I miss you.

Dad, I'm grateful for the opportunity
to spend more time with you. I love you.

TABLE OF CONTENTS

Golf is deceptively simple and endlessly complicated; it satisfies the soul and frustrates the intellect. It is at the same time rewarding and maddening — and it is without a doubt the greatest game mankind has ever invented.

ARNOLD PALMER

You can think of life as a game — like a game of golf. In life there are always obstacles to overcome, as in golf there are trees to clear, bunkers to avoid, and water to negotiate.

JACK NICKLAUS, *GOLF AND LIFE*

INTRODUCTION

Men: Read This First

I'd like to congratulate you on picking up this book. I'm sure the word GOLF got your attention and the rest captured your curiosity. Did you recently buy a new putter or driver for yourself? Did you bring back anything for your wife or significant other? This book will help her understand your love for the game in a way that has never been done before.

My personal suggestion is that you read the book first. Your loved one is likely to ask you if you've read it. You are way ahead of the game if you read it first and *then* give it to her.

In my research, I've found that men really want their wives or significant others to understand why they love the game of golf. They want them to understand the passion, excitement, and challenge they get from the game. Most of all, they really want them to know that they would love to play more often. However, your loved one may already be jealous of the time you spend on the course or even watching the game of golf. Part of the reason could be that she doesn't understand your love for the game.

Have you ever sat down and talked to her about why you love the game? You may or may not want your wife playing golf with you – that's up to you. However, the lack of communication about your love for the game will only lead you to be reminded that men are from Mars and women are from Venus. Enhanced communication has the unique ability to improve your relationship.

In his best-selling book *Mars and Venus Together Forever,* John Gray said, "Men really are seeking ways to make women happy and are just as interested as women in improved relationships." The problem he describes is that their traditional ways of doing so isn't getting through to the women. Hence the reason both men and women need to get on the same course... I mean the same page.

In this book, I will share the results from a survey conducted with men just like you. You will also learn new ways to enjoy the game of golf and reap its benefits. So, whether you are a golf fanatic playing every chance you get or more of a weekend enthusiast, sit back and enjoy a book that is going to tell you absolutely nothing about how to swing your club but could improve your game on and off the course.

We may not always see eye to eye,
but we can try to see heart to heart.

SAM LEVENSON

INTRODUCTION

Ladies: Read This First

Ladies, if you bought this book for yourself, kudos to you for being curious and wanting to learn more. If your husband or significant other has given you this book, congratulations to both of you. Why? Because this book is about more than just golf. Make no mistake, there are thousands of books about golf. However, in this book, both men and women can learn to create a level of understanding around the game of golf that can enhance their relationship and improve their outcomes on and off the course.

The man in your life wants you to understand why he loves the game of golf – but of course loves you more. Your man may or may not be good at articulating how he "feels." Remember, ladies, we're the ones who typically like to talk about everything; it's part of our nature. It's very possible that he has never told you exactly why he loves golf so much. Unfortunately, it's also possible that you've never asked him. Ahhhh, this is the making of a communication trap that we often find ourselves in with our loved ones.

In this book, you will gain a better understanding about how men look at the game of golf. In addition, you will learn how to improve your relationship and how to make more time for yourself, your friends, and your family. Who wouldn't want that? You'll also get an opportunity to explore the game of golf with a fresh pair of eyes. You will be able to look at golf not just as a sport but as a way of connecting with others and creating more "lifestyle" benefits. Finally, I'll share with you how I began to explore the golf journey. You'll learn how I went from thinking golf was a silly game that took up too much time to someone who could enjoy the "golf lifestyle."

If you are already a golfer, my hope is that you will be even more energized about the sport and find new ways to invite other women to experience the game of golf. However, the focus of this book is for those women who up until this point have had little interest in the game, have never golfed, or perhaps tried it and gave it up because they didn't have enough time.

I decided to write this book when I realized that there was an important message about the game of golf and how it pertained to life, relationships, and family. At first, I was jealous of all the time my husband spent on the golf course or watching it on TV. In talking with other women, I realized I wasn't alone. Not surprisingly, I found that men and women got different things from the game. Many of us didn't understand the game very well, and some of us had never even set foot on a golf course. How could we possibly understand the male perspective on the game and its beauty?

You may find some of the male insights from the research humorous, surprisingly deep, or in some cases, even a little crass. Men and women look at things differently, but learning from each other becomes a critical skill set in successful relationships.

Remember the book *Men Are from Mars, Women Are from Venus*? Male golfers have their own perspective and may also be from Mars. I will share my insights – not just from the research I did but also from what I have learned from growing up with golfers and then marrying one. Grab yourself a cup of tea, a comfortable chair, and dare to find some quiet time to read to your heart's content. Good luck, ladies, and may the force be with you.

THE POEM WE WANT *HIM* TO WRITE

My wife is good, my wife is great
Meeting her was worth the wait.

Let's give thanks for the love we share
Without her, life would not compare.

Her beauty is a sight to see
Her love for me is the key.

My love is strong, my commitment is true
I have treasured her since I said, "I do."

My wife is good, my wife is great
I'm leaving the 19th hole; I don't want
    to be late!

15

PART ONE

GOLF: THE GREATEST
GAME EVER PLAYED

Don't play too much golf.
Two rounds a day are plenty.

HARRY VARDON

The object of golf is not just to win.
It is to play like a gentleman and win.

PHIL MICKELSON

Chapter One

PASSION FOR THE GAME

There was a movie that came out in 2005 entitled *The Greatest Game Ever Played* – a golf drama based on a true story that occurred during the 1913 U.S. Open, where a twenty-year-old amateur, Francis Ouimet, defeated his idol, the 1900 U.S. Open champion Harry Vardon. I highly recommend this movie. It's a heartwarming story that provides an insight into a young boy's passion for the game.

It has been reported that the game of golf has been around since the fifteenth century. However, in the Middle Ages there were several games that involved hitting a ball with a stick. The earliest known reference to golf dates back to 1457, when King James II of Scotland banned golf and football on the basis that they were keeping his subjects from focusing on their archery practice. The ban was repeated in 1471 by James III and again in 1491 by James IV for the same reason.

The first surviving written reference to golf mentions St. Andrews, Scotland, and is contained in Archbishop Hamilton's Charter of 1552. St. Andrews is considered to be the "Home of Golf." In fact, as early as 1691, the town became known as the "metropolis of golfing."

Once viewed as an exclusive sport for men, golf is also a favorite pastime of women around the world. Mary, Queen of Scots is reported to be the first known woman golfer, and it has been said that she coined the term "caddie." Mary, Queen of Scots was an avid golfer; she was even criticized for playing too soon after the death of her second husband.

According to the National Golf Foundation, there are 28.6 million golfers age six and above. Only 5.8 million of them are female. As you can see, even today it is a male-dominated sport.

Let's look at the sport itself. Golf is not a contact sport (with the exception of the club making contact with the ball). It is one of the only games where you strive to get the lowest score. It is a game where a seventy-year-old can beat a seventeen-year-old, and there is no age limit on either end. It is the only sport where you call a penalty on yourself. From professionals to weekend enthusiasts, the game has a magical spell for those who love the game. While some can't put it into words, others can't wait to tell you why they love golf. Regardless, one thing is for sure: passion for golf is real, and it is easy to spot.

There are thousands of books on golf, from "how-to" books to the inspirational and the humorous. The one thing they all have in common is passion for the game. I realize that people are passionate about other sports, but there is something magical about golf for those that play the game. The next time you are at a golf course or run into a golfer, stop them and ask them why they love golf. I did this randomly every chance I got. While some were surprised by what I was asking, perfect strangers were able to articulate their answers without hesitation.

So why is there such a fascination with golf? From the everyday "Joe" or "Susie" to celebrity entertainers, CEOs, and presidents of the United States, passion for golf abounds. According to *USA Today,* fourteen of the past seventeen presidents were golfers. (In case you are wondering, Herbert Hoover, Jimmy Carter, and Harry Truman were not golfers.)

In *First Off the Tee,* a book about American presidents and golf, author Don Van Natta, Jr., wrote that Calvin Coolidge was one of the worst golfing presidents and JFK was the best. He also cited that Dwight Eisenhower was the most dedicated. It was said that he left cleat marks on the wooden floorboards of the Oval Office.

Interestingly, in the section of his book called "Hail to the Cheats," he features the golfing escapades of Bill Clinton, Richard Nixon, Lyndon Johnson, and Warren Harding.

Some of the male celebrities who play the sport for enjoyment include Clint Eastwood, Jack Wagner, Bill Murray, Matthew McConaughey, Dennis Quaid, Andy Garcia, Samuel Jackson, Justin Timberlake, Ray Romano, Kevin Costner, George Lopez, Jack Nicholson, Will Smith, Kurt Russell, Kenny G, Vince Gill, Michael Douglas, Matt Lauer, and even Alice Cooper, to name a few. Of course we can't forget the previous generation of recreational golfers like Frank Sinatra, Bob Hope, and Bing Crosby (who never missed an opportunity to play).

Some of the women celebrities who enjoy the game include Catherine Zeta-Jones, Jane Seymour, Anne Murray, Celine Dion (she owns her own golf course in Quebec), Vera Wang (she learned the game at age twelve, plays with her two daughters, and describes golf as one of the twelve things she can't live without), Sharon Stone, Mary Hart, and many others.

Sam Snead and Ben Hogan are a couple of golfing greats who turned pro in the 1930s. Then, of course, you have Arnold Palmer, Jack Nicklaus, and Gary Player, all legends and champions. Arnie and Jack were the golfers I remember my dad talking about when I was growing up.

Today there are golf greats like Tiger Woods and Phil Mickelson, who are ranked number one and two in the world at this point in time. Tiger Woods was also the first billion-dollar athlete.

There are far too many champions to mention them all. However, I would be remiss if I didn't mention a few of the women champions like Kathy Whitworth, Nancy Lopez, and Annika Sorenstam. Kathy has had eighty-eight career victories, Nancy has had forty-eight, and Annika has had seventy-two. The Ladies Professional Golf Association has twenty-three player members in the LPGA Hall of Fame and one honorary member (now deceased), Dinah Shore.

No question, golf has captured the hearts of many. Let's put aside the *Who's Who* of golfers – what about your man? Why does he love golf? In the next chapter, we'll take a look at some of the survey responses.

A GOLFER'S PRAYER

Golf is good, golf is great
For my next tee time I can hardly wait.

Let's give thanks for the links today
In the name of Ben Hogan,
  who showed us the way.

The beautiful landscape is a sight to see
And I love the feeling I get when
  I hit it off the tee.

Being with friends is the best
I'm having fun now and later I'll rest.

Golf is good, golf is great
I'm addicted; it's my fate.

When I get out on that green carpet called a fairway and manage to poke the ball right down the middle, my surroundings look like heaven on earth.

JIMMY DEMARET

Chapter Two

HONEY, HERE'S WHY I LOVE GOLF

The first person I sent my survey to was one of my colleagues. He was an avid golfer with a group of about thirty golfers he emailed every week to confirm their golf connections for the following week. I asked him to send the survey to his buddies, and he agreed. After I sent him the survey and he looked it over, he sent me the following reply.

I CAN'T SEND THIS TO MY FRIENDS –

It's too soft...

They will only answer True/False questions or multiple choice.

They will not provide paragraphs and descriptions, etc.

Good Luck!

The survey I sent had ten questions; one was multiple-choice, and the remainder open-ended. I did that because I wanted to hear "their" words in the comments. Isn't it funny that my friend was certain his buddies wouldn't fill it out? Isn't that classic Men Are from Mars, Women Are from Venus behavior? While it's true that some men wouldn't take the time, my friend was assuming that men wouldn't fill in information, only check off boxes. In reality, we did have a lot of men willing to fill in the blanks on the survey. In fact, some golfers were quite detailed in their responses – almost as if they really wanted to be heard. In addition to the electronic survey, we researched hundreds of written comments and did "on the spot" face-to-face interviews with golfers.

Assumptions can get us into trouble. I wonder, when communicating with the opposite sex, how often we are looking for more than a true/false, yes/no answer. It seems that women typically want a deeper discussion and men sometimes are more than content to give a one- or two-word answer. Classic gender communications, don't you think?

In our anonymous survey, here is what some male golfers had to say when asked what they most wanted their wives or significant others to know about why they love the game of golf:

What do you want your loved one to know about why you love the game of golf?

- I enjoy the game and have developed a passion for it. It's my paradise place where I can just enjoy the fresh air, perfect my swing, focus on getting my putter to do what it was designed to do, and have a few laughs with my buddies – and then, of course, there is always the 19th hole! Brunch and beers!

- I need time to myself with my friends.

- The stress relief and emotional refreshment benefit not only me but all those around me.

- To successfully hit a small ball over a great distance and make the par putt into a little hole is a great accomplishment. I also enjoy how every course is different, and most are a beautiful fusion of nature and landscape architecture.

- I enjoy the mental/physical challenge of the game; the experience of getting to enjoy the outdoors; fellowship with the other players in the group, even if I just met them that day.

- Getting some exercise and challenging my physical abilities.

- The scenic beauty of golf courses. The camaraderie with friends. The desire to play better, but more importantly to have fun.

- It helps me to be more balanced socially versus professionally.

- A way to be competitive with myself and others.

- Golf is a love/hate relationship; you always love the game but often don't like it when you're playing badly; it could be compared to a lifelong marriage.

- It is the most challenging sport I have ever been involved in. It is a wonderful opportunity to be outdoors in a beautiful setting.

- It is a total escape from all worry and stress.

- The challenge becomes an endless quest for perfection and keeps me coming back.

- It is fun, challenging, and I can play it basically all of my life.

- Golf is competitive; you can always improve and you always know the score.

- Time away from work, fresh air, and touching Mother Earth.

- It beats yard work; I love the fact that there are no "honey-dos" when I am playing golf.

- The feeling you get when you hit the perfect shot.

- Fresh air, exercise, scenery.

- Getting the lowest score.

- Golf gives me the opportunity to separate from daily challenges and worries. It allows me to connect with nature and enables me to reconnect with the things that really matter.

- It's an opportunity for fellowship with four like-minded people in a beautiful setting while playing a game that gives you the illusion of control over a little ball… that just keeps opening up new challenges and playing with your sanity.

- It is a good social and business activity for me.

- Has the ability to slow my mind down and help my body and spirit take a short vacation. This is greatly needed today, especially for men who are driven.

The list goes on and on; however, I did notice a few common themes. The men loved being outside in beautiful scenery, they found it a great way to take their mind off their worries, and they really enjoyed the male camaraderie – and particularly they enjoyed the challenge. You can almost see the smile on their faces as they talk about golf.

In another survey question, I asked them to list three adjectives that described the game. Here are some of the words that came up:

Passion, patience, perseverance, challenging, inconsistent, great, fun, frustrating, relaxing, alluring, historic, enjoyable, dedicated, humbling, memorable, difficult, satisfying, addictive, rewarding, Zen, impossible, funny, exhilarating, rejuvenating, amazing, soulful, nurturing, peaceful, quiet, a walk in the park, pressure, determination, emotional, refreshing, competitive, wow, awesome, incredible.

Interestingly enough, the words like "frustrating" and "enjoyable" were often paired together. It is evident that the challenge of the game is always present, but what most men take away from the game in the end is usually something positive. If you look at some of the words, ladies, you might think these men were describing a spa retreat (rejuvenating, soulful, peaceful, relaxing). As we all know, each of us experiences things in our own way. There is no one way to enjoy the game of golf.

Jack Nicklaus, in his book *Golf and Life*, talks about what comes to mind when presented with the following list of words: history, travel, nature, inspiration, friendships, etiquette, honesty, integrity, respect, courtesy, camaraderie, goodwill. He was talking about golf.

One thing is for sure, the passion runs deep for your golfer. It is important to at least try to understand that passion if you want to have a successful relationship.

Another survey question was, "Does your wife or significant other ever get jealous of your time on the golf course?" This one was also interesting. The answers were all over the board. Some said yes, some no, and – believe it or not – some were not sure. If you don't know, that would be a sure sign of a lack of communication.

Here are some of the responses (ladies, you just can't make this stuff up!):

Does your wife or significant other ever get jealous of your time on the golf course?

- No, my wife is a saint...proof that she has put up with me for forty years now.

- Yes – she thinks I'm out having fun. She just wants to spend more time with me, and I can't blame her for that.

- Sometimes it seems so. Probably because I was out having a good time and she wasn't. Not my fault.

- No. It's important to me – therefore, important to her.

- Of course, she often treats golf like some kind of a mistress that she thinks I'm cheating with.

- No, she loves me and knows that I enjoy it.

- Absolutely, because she thinks it's time that I could be doing errands, chores, etc.

- Probably some, because golf takes so long to play. But then again, so does shopping.

- Not really at this stage, because she plays too and understands the appeal.

- My first wife resented my golf, but my second wife accepts that golf is a part of my life and works around my schedule without complaint. I don't go on about her knitting and she still gets to golf with me a couple of times a month.

- I am blessed… she encourages me to play more because of the effect she sees that it has on me.

- I don't think so – I think she enjoys me being out of the house.

- No – she's usually playing with me! I'm one of the lucky ones!

- No, her father was a 10 handicapper… and seeing me play reminds her of positive images of her father… which plays to my advantage.

You can tell from the responses that some men sound like they have great relationships and others sound like they are not communicating fully with their loved ones. One of my favorite comments above was, "No, she knows it is important to me – therefore, important to her." I think that statement says it all. It doesn't require years of therapy to figure out that if something is important to someone, we would want that person to be happy and we would value that. It's not that they want to be away from us (or at least we hope not); it's just that men and women often have different interests and that is okay.

I'll give you an example. I love music. I love to play music, write music, sing, go to musicals, etc. My husband also loves music, but we don't always listen to the same kind of music. In fact, he really doesn't like going to musicals, but on occasion he will go with me because it is important to me. It's really the same concept. Different interests – different likes and dislikes.

Some men enjoy playing golf with their spouses. Others find that they need the challenge of their male counterparts. The following survey question reflects this concept.

What do you get from golfing with your male friends that you can't get when golfing with a woman?

- I'm more competitive with the same sex.
- Male bonding, the ability to use some salty language without apologizing.
- Feelings don't get hurt when the verbal barbs fly.
- I can be more open with men.
- Nothing, it would be the same.
- Not much difference. It's not the gender of the person; it's the soul.
- Men socialize with each other differently than they do with women. Golf is a vehicle for that.

- Different jokes
- Truthfully, I love playing with women, as their demeanor and their steady approach is very complementary to how I play.
- Talking about men things, such as women
- Never having to say I am sorry!
- The openness to use a four-letter word with gusto!
- A comfortable lack of political correctness. It's a tavern on the green without drinks but lots of banter and fun.
- I enjoy playing with women if they know how to play.
- Men use to go out and hunt in groups. Obviously, those days have passed. However, I'm not certain that the need to do things together as men has evaporated. There's just something about getting a foursome together, going out on the golf course, and having a great time. That cannot be captured in any other way in today's world.
- Male bonding, telling lies, and bragging.
- Male camaraderie. I don't expect a woman to understand it, nor should she have to.
- Man time!

Ladies, this list repeated itself a lot. The male-bonding issue was big. The research showed that while some men do enjoy playing golf with women, many still like that special "man time."

One of my favorite questions on the survey was the following:

Is there anything you have learned from golf that would improve your relationship?"

- Be calm, no matter what the shot or outcome is.

- Practice, practice, practice – you never know when you will get a clean shot at the hole, and you need to be ready.

- Patience pays off; work on rhythm in life, not strength.

- Patience and respect. It takes time and patience in mastering and improving your game as is true in improving a relationship. You respect golf because of its beauty and difficulty; a woman deserves respect!

- No.

- Shut up and don't offer any advice.

- Be more patient; as time goes by, things will work their way out.

- Rules to live by.

- Learning to maintain inner peace while facing a challenge.

- No round of golf is perfect, just like a relationship with your spouse. Some days there are more double bogies than others.

- Be patient, and make sure to have fun.

- Just like marriage, golf is made up of relationships – you have to work at it.

- Without tremendous suffering, there can be no progress.

- You're going to do it over and over again until you get it right.

- Not to take certain things too seriously.

- Don't cheat! Work hard.

- Don't try too hard. Ease up. Don't worry about the score. Just try to play well and have fun.

- After it's over... LET IT GO!

- I've actually learned not to get so frustrated when things don't go my way... I used to be so intense and quite often I'd finish a round and not be happy. Now I try to stay competitive, but I don't let things frustrate me as much, and I try to carry that into my day-to-day life.

- Things always change, which is good, but how prepared are you to hit the next shot? Life is heavy stuff.

- Nothing's fair, and you can't control your good or bad breaks.

- Attention to detail.

- I think two of golf's greatest lessons are persistence and patience. I can't imagine any marriage that would not be improved if the husband were more persistent in improving the marriage and more patient with his partner.

- Knowing when to play it safe.

- Golf reveals character. People who cheat in golf will cheat in other areas. So, don't cheat. Golf doesn't improve with practice unless it is good practice. It's the same with marriage. Just spending more time with my spouse won't improve my score unless I play that relationship well... consistently. You work at golf; you must work at love.

• Anything you want to be good at takes work and practice.

• Yes! The ability to share not only the good things in life but also the bad... There are some days that you will be a winner, and there are some days you won't. It's the same in a relationship; you cannot be "right" all the time... there are times you have made mistakes and must learn to not only accept them but learn from them. The ability to know that no one in the world has been built "perfectly"... we all come with flaws, just like on the course. The people who succeed in a relationship are the people who realize this and share the same sentiment with their partners.

Ladies, that entire last comment was from one person. Don't you just want to give that guy a hug for "getting it"? More importantly, can you imagine a guy taking the time to write out all that in a survey? I commend him.

The survey results gave me a new level of understanding about the game. I think you can agree from reading some of the comments that our male golfers can be quite deep in their philosophical thinking about golf and love.

In the survey, I asked the men how often they played per year — and how often they wished they could play per year. (Keep in mind that the golfers I surveyed were not professional golfers.)

Unanimously, every answer doubled the number. If it was fifteen, they wanted to do thirty; if it was fifty, they wanted to do a hundred. I think it is safe to assume most men would like to play more.

My husband's response was also double. I thought he already played a lot, but now I realize that he would like to play twice as much. This survey gives us a better understanding of just how much men really do love the game.

What I have realized from all of this is that my husband, along with the other men surveyed, gets something he needs from the game of golf. As women, we can choose to be jealous of their time on the course, be supportive of their favorite pastime, get in the game ourselves, or pretend that we don't notice.

One of the first keys to a healthy and nurturing relationship is to be supportive of your partner's love for the game. Perhaps to learn more about the game would be a good first step. Whether you choose to take up golf yourself is entirely up to you.

Many men and women enjoy playing golf together, but some men would not be without their "men only" golf outings. And many women, like myself, have found golf to be a great recreational opportunity to connect with women and enjoy the same kind of camaraderie that our men have described.

What Does All This Mean?

At this point it is pretty obvious that our men love golf, perhaps even more than we women realized. The question is, what are we doing about it? Are we striving to be more understanding and learn more about the game? Do we show that we care?

It comes back to the basics of communication. In my training and consulting business, I talk about the importance of communication in all my presentations. For example, it is impossible to talk about leadership, customer service or collaboration if you don't talk about communication. Communication skills are the most sought-after skills both personally and professionally. The lack of these skills has led to job loss, divorce, and even misunderstandings on the golf course or at home.

So here we are, talking about golf and relationships between men and women. Is it possible that communication is again the missing link? A friend of mine told me that her husband wouldn't tell her when he was playing golf because he didn't want her to know, thinking she would want him to be doing something else. She never said that; he just "assumed" it.

When my friend discovered this, she told her husband that she much preferred honesty, and she learned how important his golf time was to him. She then started to notice that when he came back from golf he was more fully present and attentive to her. As men and women, we often assume things about how each other feels, and this can get us in trouble.

I wonder how many times these misunderstandings occur and how long it takes for some couples to figure them out.

Golf and relationships – they both take work, patience, and attention to detail. But most of all, they both can be fun. In the next chapter, you will get a feel for what he wishes he could tell you about all he has learned from golf.

One thing is certain: Golf is a many-splendored thing, and so is LOVE.

A TIP FOR YOU

Let him share with you his passion for the game. Take time to understand the game. Don't just ask him what he shot that day on the course. Try this instead: "What was your best hole of the day, and what made it great?" That opens the dialogue and is far more interesting than just knowing his score.

PART TWO

WHAT YOU CAN LEARN FROM GOLF

Indeed, the highest pleasure of golf may be that on the fairways and far from all the pressures of commerce and rationality, we can feel immortal for a few hours.

COLMAN McCARTHY

Chapter Three

WHAT *HE* WISHES HE COULD TELL YOU

While this might be a bit tongue-and-cheek, consider what your male golfer might say to you if he was trying to convince you of the worth of the game. While this may appear like he is buttering you up to gain your understanding, remember that he is! That's how much he wants you to be on board with his love for the game.

Honey, when I play golf, it is hard for me to explain how I feel. I know you think that sometimes I play too much. However, I want you to consider how it keeps me in shape when I walk the course. Secondly, I want you to consider how it makes me a better partner. Yes, that's right, a better partner. I'd like to share with you what I have learned from the game of golf. However, as you read this, please know that nothing can take the place of you, not even GOLF!

Being in a relationship takes good communication, discipline, skill, and the willingness to look at your strengths and weaknesses.

Good Communication

In golf, I communicate with my golfing foursome. We don't gossip or have trivial conversation, but we support each other. When someone makes a good shot, we don't hold back. We say, "Good shot," even if we are a bit jealous. Sure, we joke and have fun on the course, but I really value the camaraderie.

Have you noticed how excited I am to leave when I am heading to the course? I don't like being away from you; I just enjoy the game. We all have hobbies or activities that we enjoy. I can play for hours and never get tired. By the way, honey, did I tell you how great you look today?

Discipline

It also takes a lot of discipline to play golf because it is not an easy game. In fact, it can be very frustrating at times when you're not playing well.

I've definitely had to learn patience and perseverance. Remember the time I threw my club and broke it? Well, while that was, of course, childish, I have since learned restraint and the importance of discipline in the game of golf (most of the time, anyway). At least I didn't wrap it around a tree like my buddy! By the way, that stress relief toy rubber club you gave me has helped a lot.

A Willingness to Look at Strengths and Weaknesses

We all know that in a good relationship we need to understand our strengths and weaknesses. For example, I'm better at some things around the house and you're better at others, but we work together in the relationship to put our individual talents to good use.

In golf, some of us need to work more on our short game and others on our long game. While it is important to look at our strengths and challenges, some things require more work than others. For example, if my strength is in putting and my short game, then I need to spend more time on my long game and getting the ball off the tee. That, of course, explains why I always want to go to the driving range. I want to get better at my game, just the way I want to focus on making our relationship better and better. Have I told you lately that I love you? I know, I just don't say those things enough.

Skill

All golfers will tell you that golf is truly a game of skill. Yet what they don't always tell you is that, deep down inside, a lot of golfers want to improve their score, lower their handicap, and just maybe one day try out for the US Open (or at least dream about it). You and I both know that relationships take skill, and I want you to know that as much as I want to improve my golf score, I want even more to put in the time and skill it takes to keep our relationship moving in the right direction.

Honey, I chose you, not golf, as my companion. Golf just happens to be an activity that I really enjoy. I know deep down that you don't really want to try and change me, and well... golf completes me and so do you. I know that sounds a little bit like something from the movie *Jerry Maguire,* but all kidding aside, with or without golf, YOU had me at "hello."

So, honey, I just wanted you to realize that golf isn't something that competes with you but something that can compliment us if we understand each other better.

A Game of Integrity: Real Golfers Never Cheat

What you might not know, honey, is that golf is really about sportsmanship and ethics. In other words, nobody in golf likes to play with a cheater. Sometimes there are those golfers that want to take their tee shot over, or they move their ball, or they forget to take a stroke penalty, or they take a "gimme" on the putting green when they should take the shot, or they even somehow miscalculate their score.

But honey, not me – I'm all about playing fair and honest. I just want you to know that not only do I not cheat in golf, but I would never cheat on you, and I believe in honesty in our relationship. Honesty is always the best policy, and I always want to be honest with you. Can you believe it, honey? I learned all this from golf. You are probably going to want me to start playing more often.

Did you know that golf is one of the only sports where you actually call a penalty on yourself? Imagine a basketball game where players called a penalty on themselves... not likely!

Golf is about integrity. Pro golfer Brian Davis was on the first play-off hole against Jim Furyk when he called a two-stroke penalty on himself that ultimately gave Furyk a victory. The violation was moving a loose impediment during a takeaway. It was described as indiscernible except for slow motion replays. That violation cost him his first PGA Tour victory. The PGA Tour tournament director Slugger White had this to say: "What Davis lost on the course will be regained in his reputation for his honorable act."

That is pretty impressive, don't you think? In golf and in life, I understand the importance of calling a penalty on yourself when it is the right thing to do.

Caring

In golf, you learn to "care"; in other words, you care about the course even though you don't own it. If I hit a shot and get a divot (sorry about the golf terminology – a divot is where the turf gets scraped up from hitting the ball), I take my tool and cover it up.

If I mess up the sand in the sand trap, I take the rake and smooth it out for the next player. I know, honey, you're probably thinking that you wish I was that conscientious around the house. Honey, I'm working on it.

It's all about caring and being responsible. Golf actually makes me a better person. I realize that all golfers might not be able to make that correlation, but then again I'm no ordinary guy. Honey, being with you makes me a better person.

Accepting "What Is"

In golf, if I hit a bad shot, I have to accept it and still move forward to improve on the next shot. I can't complain or mope about it if I want to be focused and in control for the next shot.

Love also requires couples to accept "what is." In love, we have to learn to accept each other for who we are. Instead of trying to change each other, we can learn to bring out the best in each other. Sometimes it's easy to find things we don't like in each other, but it is more rewarding to focus on the reasons we fell in love.

Neither of us is perfect, and we both have flaws. I can assure you that golf brings out the best in me (on most days). However, no one brings out the best in me like you do!

Taking Responsibility

What is interesting about golf is that it is not a competition with others; in actuality, it is a competition with myself. Some of the best players say that when they are competing they are focusing only on their game – they are trying to be the best they can be at that given moment and they're not getting caught up in where they are in relation to the other players. However, I can't deny that I like the competition, and I like winning.

Each time I play, I try to get a better score than the last time. I take full responsibility for the outcome. Just like in relationships, we both have to take responsibility for our actions. Sometimes we disagree, which is normal in any relationship. It's easy for us to blame each other when we get into a fight. Yet in the end, we both know that we are equally responsible for resolving the conflict and making the relationship stronger.

Learning from Mistakes

I make mistakes on the golf course all the time, like when I misread a green, use too much club, or go for it instead of laying up. Believe me, when I make a mistake on the course it drives me crazy, but in the end the only way I can improve is to learn from my mistakes. In relationships, we too have to learn from our mistakes, and love is sometimes "having to say you're sorry." However, one thing is for sure: I'll never be sorry I met you.

Relationships, Like Golf, Take Practice

I love to play golf and I love to go to the driving range to practice. As any golfer will tell you, it is the only way to get better. Relationships take practice too – spending time with each other, getting to know each other's likes and dislikes, learning to communicate, learning to trust each other, learning to listen, learning to talk, learning to love. I love golf, but I love "loving" you more. Practice makes perfect, don't you think?

Time to Unwind on the 19th Hole

The 19th hole is where we go after the game to unwind, have a beer, and talk about the day. Or sometimes, if we all had a bad day, we try hard *not* to talk about it. The 19th hole is a slang term referring to the pub, bar, or restaurant on or near the course. I would be remiss if I didn't tell you how much we look forward to the 19th hole. Perhaps the best way to describe it would be male bonding time and a way to unwind. Whether it is after a golf game or a hard day at work, everybody deserves to unwind.

Having You in My Life Is Like Winning the Green Jacket

The Masters Tournament (also known as the Masters) is one of the four major championships in professional golf. It is held each year at the Augusta National Golf Club in Augusta, Georgia. The winner not only gets a very large cash prize but also the infamous green jacket. The green jacket, awarded since 1949, is returned to the clubhouse after a year for the winner to wear whenever they visit. It is customary for the winner of the previous year to put the jacket on the next year's winner.

When the winner puts on the green jacket, I can only imagine that it is an amazing feeling. It's the pinnacle of success. Yet the jacket is just a symbol of that success.

In our life, there are all sorts of symbols of our love. For example, our wedding rings are a symbol of our love. However, a symbol is not enough to sustain a relationship, just like the green jacket will not sustain a player's success. It's just a temporary thing; it does not guarantee future successes. For us, our rings don't guarantee the success of our marriage. It's the day-to-day things that matter – the little things we do for each other; the "I love yous" for no reason; and the give-and-take that is required. Last week, when I left early in the morning to play golf and you said, "Have a great golf game today," believe it or not, that meant a lot to me. It showed me that you cared about what is important to me. I know that I need to pay more attention to the things that are important to you too. But if we don't talk about it, this could all go unsaid.

To sum it all up for me, being with you is like that feeling of winning the green jacket – pride, excitement, accomplishment, and joy. Wearing the green jacket would be an amazing feeling for anyone, yet it is just a symbol. The good thing about relationships is that if we nurture them they become more than a feeling and evolve into an enduring love. **Honey, I love golf, but I love you more!**

AUTHOR'S COMMENTARY

I had the opportunity to watch the 2010 Masters Tournament on television. Phil Mickelson won the tournament. It was so heartwarming to see him embrace his wife Amy, who has been battling cancer. Phil had a tear rolling down his cheek, and I could just feel the emotion and the love between them. It brought a tear to my eye too. He was thrilled to win, but I couldn't help thinking that what he was really saying was, "Honey, I love golf, but I love you more." It seemed apparent to me that he clearly understood his priorities and that his marriage came first.

Doubt yourself and you doubt everything you see. Judge yourself and you see judges everywhere. But if you listen to the sound of your own voice, you can rise above doubt and judgment. And you can see forever.

NANCY LOPEZ

Chapter Four

MY STORY... A WOMAN'S PERSPECTIVE

Our men would like to convince us that golf is good for them, and the truth is it is. I've come to the conclusion that they truly value quality time with their buddies just as we value our time with our girlfriends. They also enjoy playing a sport that challenges them like no other.

So what have I learned from all of this? I come from a family of golfers. My seventy-eight-year-old dad is a golfer, my brother is a golfer with a 5 handicap, my niece got a scholarship to play golf in college, my husband is an avid golfer, and even one of my closest friends is on a ladies' golf league.

I was late coming to the game – very late, you might say. For many years I just thought it was silly to hit a tiny ball around for four to five hours, and it just didn't appeal to me. I could think of a million other ways to spend my time. My husband played on a regular basis, yet I never understood his infatuation with the game.

As my daughter got a little older and became involved in more activities, it seemed that quality family time was becoming rare. There were so many things to do, so many school and work activities, and so little time to regroup as a family.

My husband always spent quality time with our daughter and he is an excellent dad, but we were finding that we were each doing separate activities with our daughter on different days, quite by accident. For example, if my husband golfed on Saturday, then my daughter and I would do our activities together on Saturday. On Sunday, he'd want to do something fun with her, and I'd find myself needing to stay home to catch up on work, grocery shopping, cleaning the house, or just the run-of-the-mill errands. We didn't even realize that we weren't spending that much time as a family until my daughter said one day, "We never have any time together with all three of us."

So we started to focus on ways we could fit in "family time," yet not be stressed over all the things that didn't get done. I have to admit that there are some things around the house that I felt I did better, so I just took them on. This is a trap we women put ourselves in by thinking we need to be "in control" of certain things that we think only we can do. When I taught stress management, we called this the perfectionist and "do it all" syndrome, which is very dangerous and a big contributor to stress. Can any of you ladies relate?

My husband loves to play golf and I didn't ever want to deprive him of that; however, I often found myself jealous of the time he spent on the course. He didn't abuse it, but it did eat up a good portion of the weekend from time to time. Then one summer, just before my birthday, I told my husband that I wanted to take up golf. Guess what? I got clubs for my birthday. In fact, both my daughter and I got clubs that year.

I enrolled my daughter in a golf camp to get acquainted with the game, and I took some lessons myself. I would go to the driving range and hit balls, and surprisingly, it was quite fulfilling. However, somehow the hustle and bustle of being a mom took its toll, and quite unintentionally, golf disappeared again from my radar. Other things just took priority, and I didn't miss it for about two years. My husband still continued to play, but I just couldn't commit to the time myself. Later, I realized that part of the reason it dropped off my radar was that I didn't have a group of women at my level to play with (more on this later).

It was at this point that I started to question myself. Why had I become so enthused about golf and then lost interest so quickly? In my research, I discovered that this was not uncommon and that there were a lot of women who didn't stick with the game. Keep in mind; we are not talking about the pros, just recreational golfers.

As noted earlier, only about 25 percent of the golfers are women. So without debate, we can safely say it is a more popular sport among men. But why is that? I started asking women who played golf why they played, and then I asked other women why they quit. In addition, I asked nonplayers why they never considered taking up the sport. Here are some of their responses.

Women's Responses

Why do you like to play golf?

- I play golf because it's good for business.
- I enjoy the game, and my husband and I play together.
- I love the beautiful scenery.
- It gives me time to think and relax.
- I like to get together with my girlfriends.
- It's challenging.
- I belong to a golf club.

Why did you stop playing golf?

- I quit because I just didn't have the time.
- It takes up too much of my day.
- I didn't have any friends who played.
- I lost interest before I really understood the game.
- It took too much time away from my family.

Why didn't you ever take up the game of golf?

- I never started because I didn't have anyone to play with and didn't want to go out on my own.
- It never interested me.
- I don't know much about the game.
- I never tried it.

- I like watching it on TV, but it looks very complicated.

- Hitting a little white ball around for five hours doesn't
  sound like fun.

As far as why most women gave up the game of golf, more often than not it came down to time. At this point, I started looking at golf a little differently.

First, I began thinking about how much fun it would be if my husband and I had a hobby in common. Particularly when we retired, it would be ideal. Secondly, I thought it could be a great family hobby for the three of us — real quality time together. Lastly, I realized that golf was a great sport to enjoy with other girlfriends.

My Journey Back to Golf

I started playing golf again this past year. My first trip out was to a 9-hole, par 3 course to give my daughter and I a chance to refresh ourselves about the game. This particular par 3 was an easy course for my husband. He didn't even bring his golf bag. He just grabbed a putter, a 7 iron, and a sand wedge. My daughter and I grabbed our bags and began the journey.

What happened this time was that I took a different approach. I didn't let my mind wander about all the things I should be doing, or what I was going to do after we finished golf. I simply participated in the moment. What a gift it is to be in the present moment! Eckhart Tolle's book, *The Power of Now*, talks about the importance of being in the "now" and fully present. I ask you, is it possible that you are depriving yourself of being in the now? It's true that many of us are master multitaskers. I've decided to become a recovering multitasker. While multitasking does come in handy, it often deprives us of being in the NOW.

On this particular day, on that 9-hole course I was fully present and in the now. How wonderful it was! I paid attention to the game and to what I was doing, even when my ball didn't always go in the direction I intended. It didn't matter. It was a beautiful day – 80 degrees, blue skies – and the scenery on the course was lovely. I noticed every detail, from the blades of grass and the ducks that decided to land anywhere they wanted to an appreciation for a sand trap and the lake that my ball seemed to enjoy.

Afterward, we stopped in at the course café and had a sandwich together. I left that day feeling that my time had been well spent. We all had a great time. In addition, it was a stress-buster, and I got to enjoy the exercise from walking the course. The 9-hole course only took us about an hour and a half, which was perfect. It's true that I could have spent an hour working out, but I wouldn't have been with my family, and I probably wouldn't have been in the NOW. Par-3 courses are a great place to start when you are learning and building up to the 18-hole courses.

So what did I learn from that day on the golf course? First of all, I don't always have to play 18 holes. Sometimes 9 holes will work nicely. However, keep in mind that for men it's not the same. They still feel the need to play the more complicated 18-hole courses. In fact, my husband and his friends once played 36 holes of golf in one day. That's hard for me to even imagine, but they had a blast and couldn't wait to do it again. Secondly, what made this day so special was that I was with my family, and I was able to be in the moment to enjoy the game, the scenery, and the company.

To get better at golf, I knew I would need to play more. I also knew that my husband still needed his time on the golf course with his male friends. This didn't mean that we couldn't play together occasionally, but I now understood his need to play with his male foursome. I would need to be proactive in order to find other women at my level to play the game with.

I mentioned golf to one of my girlfriends, and she said she wanted to try it some time. Her dad was a golfer, but she has never picked up a club. She makes time for bunco but had never made time for golf... yet! She said, "I don't know if I will like it or not because I've never tried, but I'm willing to give it a go."

I know a lot of women who play bunco, which is a simple game of dice. It is so simple that women can roll the dice and not concentrate on the game. What they really want to do is get together and talk, which is why bunco is referred to as a social dice game. It is reported that there are over 27 million women who play bunco! Keep in mind, there is no exercise or fresh air involved in bunco.

While golf does take focus and concentration, you still have an opportunity to converse. At the end of the game, there is always the opportunity to get together and have lunch or a glass of wine and connect with your friends. However, you have to try it first to discover this for yourself. The bottom line is that we make time for anything we decide is important to us.

Women love the camaraderie on the course as much as men do. It's possible that our conversations may not be as sports-directed as our male counterparts. We may not analyze every shot, and most certainly we won't talk about the game through our entire lunch. But that's okay – who ever said men and women were alike? One thing is certain: we need to take more initiative to carve out that time for our women friends.

Everybody Has a First Time –
Jimmy's Story

I realized that just getting started with something new can be intimidating, but everyone has a first time. A twelve-year-old boy named Jimmy back in the 1940s had a group of friends, all of whom were caddies at the local golf club. Jimmy didn't know anything about golf, but he showed up at the course one day with his buddies. As it turned out, they were short a caddie that day. They told Jimmy to go down to the caddie shack and they would call him by name over the PA when they were ready. He said to one of his friends, "What do I do? I don't know anything about golf." His friend replied, "Don't worry, it's easy. I'll be up ahead; just keep your eye on where the ball goes."

After the first tee shot, the golfer's ball went into the rough. Jimmy ran toward the ball, picked it up, and handed it to the golfer, politely saying, "Here it is, sir, here's your ball." You're never supposed to touch the ball, but Jimmy didn't know that. He remembered getting a scolding that day from the golfer and heard him say to his partner, "I've got a handful with this kid."

Let's just say that Jimmy learned a lot about the game that day. Remember, everyone has a first day. Jimmy went on to caddie for many years, and this led to his love for the game.

Jimmy remembers caddying for a private country club in Creve Coeur, Missouri. He used to ride his horse to Westwood Stables right next door to the club. They would keep his horse while he walked over to the course to caddie. He said it was the most beautiful course he could imagine. Years later, when he was about twenty and no longer caddying, he got dressed up and went back to the club. They thought he was there to play. He knew he couldn't play because it was a private course.

He said, "No, sir, I'd like to caddie today. I'd like to play this course one more time, and if I caddie for you today I'll be able to play the course on Monday [which was 'Caddie Day']." The starter was so impressed with how he was dressed and his initiative that he put him out there as a caddie. On Monday, Jimmy got to play the course one more time.

You never know how your love for the sport will evolve. Today Jimmy is my dad. The irony is that I never heard this story until I started writing this book. It's amazing what you can learn about people when you talk about what interests them. Once again, this validates the idea that there are opportunities to learn at every corner if you are open to the experience.

The Golf Widow

I was lucky enough to find out about a group called Women on Course, founded by Donna Hoffman. This organization focuses on connecting women to the "golf lifestyle."

I immediately connected with Donna and was amazed to hear her story. At one time she described herself as a "golf widow." She was married, balancing three small children and a full-time career as a television producer.

She said, "On Saturday mornings, my husband would leap out of bed to meet his golf buddies, only to return Sunday after dinner. After nine years, I decided to make my 'single mom' status official. After my divorce, every man I met seemed to have a fixation on golf, so I decided to be clear right up front. 'I have three small children, and golfers need not apply.' It worked... until I met Mark. I later found out he carried a 2 handicap."

Donna explains that what happened this time around was quite different. Mark introduced her to the game of golf by creating experiences he knew she would enjoy. He made sure she got a few basic lessons to master the swing (not the kind where a husband tells you to "keep your eye on the ball"). He then took her to a PGA tournament, and she loved walking the course, following the players. Donna admitted that it was when they traded a long winter weekend for a golf resort getaway that sealed the deal.

Donna said, "I shopped for sporty new outfits, spent my days in the sun, and used the course as my daily exercise. I discovered that golf is a great way to focus my mind and share quality time. We ended each day with chardonnay and a sunset... I was hooked!"

It was from that point that Donna knew she had to share her new passion. She founded Women on Course, an organization designed to introduce and connect women to the "golf lifestyle" (visit www.HoneyILoveGolf.com to get a special Women On Course membership free gift). As Donna says, the "golf lifestyle" is about living life to its fullest.

I became a Women on Course member and attended my first event, a social event at Fleming's Steakhouse. I had a wonderful lunch, a glass of wine, and an opportunity to meet some great women. In addition, there was a fashion show by Golfsmith, interactive activities, and lots of prizes. Callaway Golf actually donated two beautiful golf bags that two lucky attendees won.

This is just one type of event. There are also golfing events that get women on the golf course. These appeal to women of all skill levels, including those new to the game. For me, these types of events are a great way to spend some quality time with like-minded women and be able to enjoy not only their company but the beautiful outdoors.

From this point forward, I was hooked for a variety of reasons. Golf doesn't have to focus on competing; it can be a unique way to further develop relationships and make time for yourself in a fun way. It is important for me to share my story and Donna's because I know there are a lot of women out there who have never even considered exploring golf, or who perhaps had a bad experience.

PART THREE

FOR WOMEN ONLY

Learn to enjoy every minute of your life. Be happy now. Don't wait for something outside of yourself to make you happy in the future. Think how really precious is the time you have to spend, whether it's at work or with your family.

EARL NIGHTINGALE

Chapter Five

MAKING TIME FOR YOURSELF

Making time for yourself is not always easy. With so many things to do at home or work, it is easy to fall into the trap of eliminating all the things that pertain to your own well-being. Do you ever find yourself saying, "I'd like to, but I just don't have time?"

When you fly, the flight attendant always announces, "In the unlikely event of an emergency, please secure your oxygen mask first and then assist your child." Instinctively, mothers want to assist their child first. However, the logic behind this announcement is that you must secure your mask first because if something happens to you, then you are not available to help your child. As women, we are great at nurturing and taking care of others. However, if you don't take care of yourself it can negatively impact your life.

It is important to take care of your own health and well-being. This affects every aspect of your life, both personally and professionally. Intuitively we know this, yet it is not always easy to accomplish.

The stress that comes from being overwhelmed by too many things to do, accompanied by feeling "guilty" over not doing enough, can be taxing. When this happens, our own physical health and well-being often takes a backseat.

Part of taking care of your health and well-being includes making time for yourself. You may have several roles in your life such as wife, mother, caregiver, or business owner. Regardless of these roles, do you make time for yourself? Time to read a book, play a sport, get a pedicure, relax, or do whatever is important to you.

Each year I go on a two-day retreat in Santa Barbara alone. There are no TVs, and the setting is designed for quiet reflection. It's a great time to think, pray, read, reflect, write, plan for the future, and relax. My husband understands and encourages me to go.

Making time for yourself can also include playing golf. If you work nine-to-five or find yourself working overtime, you are probably thinking how hard it would be to put in a round of golf. However, you could hit a bucket of balls after work or play 9 holes on the weekend – or even take a lesson. This can be a great stress reliever. A round of golf, fresh air, exercise, pleasant scenery, and a little time for yourself or with friends might be just what the doctor ordered.

If you are a beginning golfer or just thinking about taking up the sport, consider these benefits:

- Golf is good exercise, especially if you walk the course.

- The scenery can be fabulous.

- Golf has been known to reduce stress.

- You can travel and play golf at beautiful resorts. (When you're done golfing with your husband you can go to the SPA – yeah!)

- If you practice being in the NOW, you will leave the course in a better place, ready to tackle any other tasks.

- You can use the time to practice gratitude. You can be grateful for your friends and family, for the beautiful landscape that God created, or even for your ability to walk the course, if that's the case. I'm also teaching my daughter to practice gratitude. It is so easy to forget how much we truly have to be grateful for.

- You can create family time on the course with your husband or significant other and your kids. Or you can create girlfriend time on the course. Imagine getting four of your good friends together as a foursome on the golf course and then enjoying lunch together afterwards. How often do we get to create that experience?

- Many men and women golf with clients. It is a very friendly, relaxed environment. Men have been doing deals on the golf course since the beginning of golf. For both men and women, in these difficult economic times it is tougher and tougher to get quality time with our clients. If you can use four hours on the course to get to know your client better, there is no doubt this is an opportunity to enhance the relationship.

Create Your Own "Back Nine Club"

Remember, if not having enough time to play is your primary issue, there is nothing wrong with playing 9 holes. Men tend to be content only if they are playing 18 holes, but either way is fine. Get a group of women together and play 9 holes and meet for drinks afterwards. If you don't have the people to play with, join one of the women golfing organizations.

There are lots of benefits to playing golf, but the decision is yours. Sometimes all it takes is a first step. For me, I find it energizing. I can play golf with my husband, talk about the sport a little better, and even watch golf on TV without having to ask too many questions. I've noticed that when men watch sports they like to do exactly that: "watch" the sport. A lot of questions can be annoying. Luckily, our remote has a "pause" button!

The bottom line is that golf is like any other sport – you can find a place for it in your life if you choose to. It may not be for everybody, but after taking a second look, I saw so many more benefits than the first time I took it up. If this sounds like you, you might want to give it another try. The important thing to remember is that you won't get better without practice, but there is nothing wrong with playing occasionally until you can create more time in your schedule. Heading to the driving range or putting green is another way to begin the golf journey.

Test Your Readiness

If the men in your life love golf, that's great – as long as they love you more! You may find that you too love GOLF! If you become the golfer and your significant other hasn't yet taken up the sport, invite him to play. As long as love and relationships come first, golf can be a win-win.

Don't base your decision to take up golf based on someone else's experience. For example, I once heard Joy Baer, cohost of *The View*, say that she thought golf was about as much fun as watching paint dry. I wonder if she has ever even tried playing, or if this was just a preconceived notion. The best thing is to try it for yourself and make up your own mind. Turn the page for a quiz you can take, followed by some ideas to get your started.

"Tell personnel to hire someone who can help me with my putting."

ARE YOU READY FOR GOLF?

- Am I in need of more quality time with my spouse or significant other?

- Do I need to spend more quality time with my family?

- Am I in need of more quality time with my girlfriends?

- Do I need to have more in common with my spouse or significant other?

- Would I like to spend more time outdoors?

- Do I have a need to learn to be in the present moment and experience the NOW?

- Do I need more exercise?

- Do I need to challenge myself more?

- Do I need to reduce my stress and improve my physical health?

- Do I need to have more fun?

If you answered yes to three or more of these questions, you may want to create a new game plan for yourself!

IDEAS TO GET YOU STARTED

1. Take a golf lesson or attend a clinic.

2. Rent or borrow some clubs if you don't have your own.

3. Spend time at the driving range or putting green.

4. Join a women's golf organization like Women on Course or the Executive Women's Golf Association. (If you are not sure which group is for you, check out one of their events and get to know them. That's what I did.)

5. Attend a golf outing or event.

6. Attend as a spectator or work at a charity golf event.

7. When you are ready, invite some friends and head out to a Par 3 course.

8. Check with your local golf course to see what they offer.

9. Take your son or daughter to the driving range, or go with your husband or a friend. (Save your marriage: Don't ask your husband for lessons – go to a pro!)

10. Have FUN!

Golf teaches you discipline and goal-setting and how to control your emotions.

SANDRA POST (WON THE LPGA CHAMPIONSHIP IN 1968 AT AGE TWENTY)

Chapter Six

BREAKING THE START/STOP SYNDROME

According to the National Golf Foundation, women make up the largest segment of new golfers. However, while new women take up golf every year, many also quit the game – usually for many of the reasons mentioned earlier, such as not enough time, or not having anyone to play with. As I mentioned, I too started, stopped, and started again. The secret is to find a group of people you want to play with or join a women's group as I did. This allows you to network, have fun, and learn about the game with absolutely no pressure.

An example comes to mind that those of you who are parents might relate to. When my daughter started an activity or sport, it was important that she finished the season before making a decision that she wanted to quit. In other words, I've always felt that if you try something new you have to stick with it for awhile to really determine if you like it.

A friend of mine signed her daughter up for volleyball because she wanted her daughter to have an activity to do after school while she was at work. The daughter cried because she didn't want to do it, but she reluctantly agreed to try it. Now she loves the sport and has become quite good at it.

My experience is that the game of golf can be similar in that if you don't give it some time, you may not get to discover just how much you enjoy it. This was definitely true for me. I have met women who are just as addicted to golf as many men I know.

These days, I am more committed to finding ways to enjoy the game. While in Hawaii on vacation, my family and I went to a beautiful golf course. We had breakfast at the restaurant overlooking the course. My husband and daughter decided they wanted to practice their putting, and I headed to the driving range on the property. I was the only woman at the driving range with the exception of a woman sitting on a bench watching. After I was done hitting balls, I walked over to the woman and began talking with her.

A few minutes later, her husband (who was hitting balls) walked over to us. Drew and Leanne were from Scotland, and they were on their honeymoon. As it turns out, Drew began playing about a year earlier. His father-in-law was always asking him to play, but he wasn't that interested. He then began playing the electronic Wii Golf game, and that's what got him interested in playing. He then got three friends interested in golf, and his journey began. Before long he was hooked. They joined a municipal course, and within a year he joined a private golf club.

He told me he wanted Leanne to play with him, but she wasn't interested. She said, "I've tried it, but I play like rubbish." Just like with Drew, it takes playing a bit to become hooked. As far as Leanne, I don't think she has played enough to really give it a chance. Perhaps she will break the "start/stop syndrome" and give it one more try.

Don't Give Up

If you go through a period where you just don't have time for the sport, don't give up; just get back in the game. Often when women haven't played in awhile, they are reluctant to get out there again because they feel they won't be any good.

I asked a friend who was an avid golfer to join me at a golfing event and if not for another obligation, she said she would have been delighted to go. I invited another friend who is more of an occasional golfer to be a guest at a Women on Course golf event. Her first comment was, "I don't know – I haven't swung a golf club in quite a while. When I explained that this particular event was a social luncheon, she was more than happy to attend. There is sometimes that reluctance to get back out there when it has been a while since you have played.

It's easy to get back into the game if you know you are not going to be judged. That's why it is easier to initially play with other women until you understand the game better. I found that in the beginning, although my husband was open to playing golf with me, he was definitely hoping I would get better at the game so I wouldn't hold him up and, more importantly, so I wouldn't have to ask him so many questions during the game and risk getting into an argument. That is why lessons, practice, and golf with the girls can prevent the start/stop syndrome and give you that time for yourself that you deserve.

Golf is so much more than getting the ball in the hole. It's an environment, a culture, a mood.

DONNA HOFFMAN, FOUNDER OF WOMEN ON COURSE

Chapter Seven

THE GOLF LIFESTYLE

The "golf lifestyle" becomes what you create for yourself. This is an opportunity to make golf a part of your life in a fun and entertaining way. As you will recall, I introduced you earlier to Donna Hoffman, the founder of Women on Course. Her passion is creating the golf lifestyle for women. Here's how Donna defines the golf lifestyle:

> "Golf is so much more than getting the ball in the hole. It's an environment, a culture, a mood. Around the golf course women can socialize and network, enjoy breathtaking scenery, escape from the pressures of everyday life, work their bodies, and learn new skills. The golf lifestyle expands the definition of participating in golf not only as a player but as a spectator or volunteer at a fund-raiser."

The beauty of golf is that many courses are on fabulous properties, many of which are resorts. These resorts are in great locations throughout the world. If you like to travel, golf is an added benefit.

After playing a round of golf, you can enjoy the sunset, a glass of wine, or an exquisite meal if you so desire. If you are at a resort, you can also enjoy the spa and other activities to top off your golf vacation.

If you get involved in a golfing organization like Women on Course, you have the opportunity to go to golfing or social events that may include spa days, wine tastings, golf fashion shows, or luncheons.

While there are some women who play golf for the competitive challenge, there are many who are looking for the opportunity to connect with others. You have the opportunity to create your own experience. Whether it's a golf date with your husband or a day out with the girls, it becomes what you make it.

Take a moment and think about what the "golf lifestyle" might look like for you, and begin to create the life you love. For me, golf, travel, and fun make for an intriguing combination.

The golf lifestyle means something different for everyone. Why not determine what it means to you? As I mentioned earlier, the golf lifestyle can include being a spectator, watching an event on television, or going to a live tournament. I have a friend who works a golf charity event for the local hospital every year, and she finds that to be a rewarding way to give back.

Women and Girls –
The Opportunity to Give Back

As women, we have a lot of things in common, and we want to support each other. For myself, I know I want to leave the world a better place than when I got here. As I began researching for this book, I stumbled upon a movement called The Girl Effect. It's a movement focused on the world's greatest untapped potential – a girl. There is an amazing social and economic change brought about when girls have the opportunity to participate in their community, society, education, health, decision-making, and family. The Girl Effect focuses on adolescent girls in developing countries that live in poverty. Their motto is "Invest in a girl, and she will do the rest." Please visit the website, view the video at www.girleffect.org, and then pass it on to others if you feel so inclined.

The Girl Effect movement has partnered with Global Giving to help fund numerous projects throughout the world. Golfers will tell you that golf is complicated, and it is true. Others tell us that life is complicated, and that can be true as well. But there is one thing that is not complicated at all – one person helping another, no matter how small or insignificant the act or deed may be. This very simple concept is often overlooked.

So what's golf got to do with this? I believe it has everything to do with it. What started as a simple book about golf and love unconsciously through my research brought me to the understanding of The Girl Effect. For me, The Girl Effect movement has helped me to realize that any of us can help other young women reach the greener fairways of life and provide them with a better chance of contributing to the world. Individuals or organizations can help by creating an awareness of the problem or by making it their philanthropic charity of choice.

There are 600 million girls living in poverty, and it is not likely that many of them will be playing golf any time soon. However, moving out of poverty is just the beginning of positive change, and we never know where that positive change will take us. As you can see, the "golf lifestyle" goes beyond just golfing and involves being connected with others in deep and meaningful ways.

There are many charity golf events throughout the world that continue to do amazing things by contributing to a wide variety of charitable organizations. In fact, the PGA (Professional Golfers' Association) charities have donated billions of dollars since its inception. The PGA Wives Association helps needy children and their families through charitable events. The LPGA (Ladies Professional Golf Association) raises money for charities through their tournaments as well. There are charity golf events going on all across the world. Getting involved in a golf charity event might be a first step to getting involved in golf.

TIPS FOR ENJOYING
THE GOLF LIFESTYLE

1. Enjoy the social and emotional satis-faction of the game.

2. Use golf to connect and bond with others.

3. De-stress by enjoying the beautiful scenery.

4. Attend a golf charity event.

5. Plan a golf vacation.

6. Have fun!

PART FOUR

FOR MEN AND WOMEN

*I love the game of golf, and I've never
lost the intense passion for sports and
sense of pure fun I had as a kid.*

ANNIKA SÖRENSTAM, *GOLF ANNIKA'S WAY*

Chapter Eight

FAMILY AND FRIENDS THAT
PLAY TOGETHER STAY TOGETHER

Golf can be a great activity for families as well. Having activities that the entire family can enjoy is often rare. Men, women, and boys and girls of all ages can enjoy golf. In an era where many families rarely eat meals together due to such hectic schedules, it's more important than ever to regain those "family" moments. Golf allows you to spend quality time with family members. This is another opportunity to create great memories that you and your family can treasure.

Play Golf America is a golf website (PlayGolfAmerica.com) that was founded to grow the game of golf. You will find helpful information about the sport on this site. They host events such as Family Golf Month, Bring Your Kids to the Golf Range, Bring Your Daughter to the Course Week, and the American Express Women's Golf Month, just to name a few. There are also things like parent-child outings that feature 6- to 9-hole events that are fun for the whole family. In addition, if you are new to golf they have a Get Golf Ready program. This site is a great resource.

There are also other types of golf organizations specifically for women, couples, youth, seniors, singles, and men. There is even an association for blind golfers, the United States Blind Golfers Association (USBGA). Golf has something for everyone. The great thing about golf is that at whatever age you discover the game, you can continue to play it into your retirement. It one of the few sports I know of that you can play when you are eighty and still enjoy it. If you don't believe me, ask Arnold Palmer.

Playing golf with your spouse, significant other, a friend, or family member can give you an opportunity to have quality time with that person. If you choose to use golf as a way to meet new people, that is another opportunity to develop new friendships. One woman took up the game of golf amidst some amazing circumstances and made a lot of new friends as she became addicted to the sport. Let's take a look at her story.

Friendships That Are Out of Sight

Can you hit a hole in one with your eyes closed? Hitting a hole in one is challenging for any golfer. But what if you are blind? Sheila Drummond is president of the United States Blind Golfers Association, and she is totally blind. It was 2007 on the 4th hole, which is a Par 3 measuring 149 yards. She hit the ball off the tee, and her husband/coach commented, "Nice shot!" Sheila said, "I think I heard it hit the pin." She was right. It hit the pin and went into the hole for an unprecedented hole in one. Sheila's husband, Keith, has never had a hole in one but has a good sense of humor.

When asked if he ever got a hole in one he now replies, "No, but I have coached a hole in one."

Within six hours, the news was all around the world. The next day she was on the *Good Morning America* show. They had a net on the set, and she had to hit some golf balls. Her first question was, "What is behind the net if I shank the ball?" They replied, "A million-dollar window." Sheila wished she had never asked the question! But she knew how to relax herself and gain the composure necessary to hit the shot. The net had a bull's eye marked on it, and all three of her shots went right into the bull's eye. Now *that's* what I call focus.

Sheila became blind when she was twenty-seven years old due to diabetic retinopathy. At age thirty-six, she met some people who told her about an association for blind golfers. Sheila had never played golf but thought it sounded interesting. She took some lessons at a local course, found a friend to coach her, and eventually went to a golf school in Florida. She was hooked. Two years later, she got her husband interested in the game, and he became her golf coach. (Every blind golfer has a sighted coach to assist them on the course. Coaches line up the ball, read the green, and are the blind golfer's eyes on the course. It really becomes a team sport at that point.)

Sheila has been golfing for seventeen years. Her best score so far for 18 holes is 106. She has broken 50 on 9 holes on either the front or the back 9 but so far hasn't put the two together to break 100. However, she hasn't ruled out the possibility that her best games are ahead of her. Sheila said that getting involved in golf and the USBGA has allowed her to meet a lot of great people that she wouldn't have met otherwise, and she has made friends that will last a lifetime.

I had the opportunity to interview Sheila about her golfing experiences. I wanted to share Sheila's story for a couple of reasons. First, her attitude about life, her willingness to try new things, and her ability to deal with change is amazing. Secondly, I felt that her story would be motivating and inspirational to any golfer, blind or not.

SHEILA'S TIP FOR THE DAY

Stay focused, practice,
and trust your coach!

FAMILY AND FRIENDS GAME PLAN

1. Introduce someone new to the game of golf.

2. Set a golf date.

3. Take a family member or friend to a PlayGolfAmerica.com event.

4. Schedule time in your calendar to go to a putting green or driving range.

5. Celebrate special events on the golf course.

Practice puts brains in your muscles.

SAM SNEAD

Chapter Nine

FIT FOR GOLF, FIT FOR LIFE

Is it possible to believe that if you are fit for golf you are fit for life? Let's just say it's a start. More importantly, any first step toward fitness is a good thing. I will be the first to admit that I really don't like exercise. It was just something that didn't appeal to me. However, as the years have crept by (I won't say how many) and I began to read more and more about the importance of exercise as it pertained to my longevity, I decided to give it a serious look.

The gym isn't for everyone. The key is to find what works for you. I enjoy walking my dog with a friend so we can walk and talk and catch up, all at the same time. However, this is not enough to really get the heart pumping, so I have started going to aerobic classes at the gym.

I was recently at my doctor's office. She asked me, "Are you exercising?" Luckily, this time I could say yes. She is an MD with two small children. I asked her how she found the time to exercise.

Her reply was, "I don't have a choice." In other words, she knew that regardless of how busy she was, her own health depended on exercise.

For me, I get bored easily. Therefore, it is better for me to have a variety of ways to get exercise. I have found that golf is one of those ways.

These Golf Shoes Were Made for Walking

Many amateur golfers choose to ride in a golf cart as opposed to walking the course. However, they are missing a big fitness benefit. Some people claim that golf is not exercise; however, common sense tells us that walking is a great way to exercise.

The American Heart Association recommends that one method to monitor your physical activity level is to achieve 10,000 steps per day. Research has shown that an average 18-hole course is the equivalent of about 10,000 to 11,000 steps. This is equivalent to about five miles. Even if you decide to play 9 holes, you still get at least 5,000 steps.

Edward A. Palank, MD, is a cardiologist at the Southwest Florida Heart Group in Naples, Florida. It is here that he merged his passion for clinical cardiology and golf. He is known as the Golf Doc and has done health segments on the Golf Channel.

In an interesting study, Dr. Palank evaluated the effects of walking the golf course. In his study, he looked at "bad" cholesterol versus "good" cholesterol. One group of middle-aged golfers walked three times a week for four months, while making no changes in their diets or starting any other exercise program. A similar control group didn't play walking golf. The walking golf-ers decreased their "bad" cholesterol, while their good cholesterol stayed about the same.

It is estimated that golfers who drive carts burn around 200 to 400 calories per 18 holes, whereas walkers can burn 700 to even 1,000 calories. This, of course, depends on your weight and the weight of your bag if you are carrying it.

Some men I know like to carry their clubs because it adds some weight-bearing exercise to their game. For me, carrying the clubs can put a little too much pressure on my shoulder. With the help of a pull cart, you can easily carry your bag without hurting your back or shoulder. You might also switch from a single-strap bag to a double-strap bag and see if that helps.

My girlfriend, who belongs to a golf country club and lives on a golf course, reminded me that some private clubs don't allow the pull carts (but they do have caddie programs). However, if you are just getting started in the game of golf, you may not belong to a club.

Walking the course is still a great choice for your health. Keep in mind that you will need to be in good shape to walk the course. If you find it difficult to walk the entire course, you could walk every other hole or walk nine, ride nine. Some people suggest that walking the course can even improve your score. Consider that you also have more time to see what lies ahead and think about the strategy for your next shot.

By the way, don't forget that hitting balls at the driving range can burn about 200 calories per hour. So whether you are hitting balls or walking 9 or 18 holes, the exercise is still good for you.

TIPS FOR HEALTHY GOLF

- Warm up for ten to fifteen minutes before playing the course.
- Stretch three times a week and target the areas that are more golf-specific, such as the back, shoulders, and arms. (Talk to a pro for a fitness program to improve your game.)
- Drink lots of water on the course to stay hydrated.

Get Your Vitamin D on the Golf Course

While walking around the links, soak up the sunshine and get some Vitamin D – it's essential to your body. But don't forget your sunscreen! That is a must. Wearing sunglasses is a good idea too.

To Stress or Not to Stress

What about playing golf to reduce stress? Some golfers find that golf reduces stress. Others who fail to master their emotions find the game stressful and frustrating. In the survey I conducted, I asked the male golfers about this, and here are some of their replies:

Have you ever thrown your golf club, and if so, was it worth it?

- No, not that type of guy.

- Yes, I have thrown clubs… yes, it was worth it because it went further than the ball.

- Yes, at that very moment it was worth it. Not worth it when you gain your senses and really think about what you did.

- No, that's what the game of golf does to you… play with your mind… the whole idea is to stay in "control" and focus on recovery rather than loss.

- No, not that serious.

- No, my troubles don't lie in the equipment.

- Yes, I threw a club into a tree once and it got stuck. I had to shake the tree branch to get it down. It was absolutely worth it. I've heard stories of people throwing their entire bags into lakes before.

- Once, and not too far. More of a fling of about three feet. Nothing like a toss into a lake. Golf is a game of emotion, and you cannot let your emotions overtake you or you will do worse.

- No, have never thrown a club. Banged it on the ground a few times, however.

- No… I believe it is disrespectful to your fellow players.

- Yes, I have. Yes, it was worth it!

- No, but I have had colorful conversations with my clubs… some I have divorced… for good reason.

- Once – damned near hit two of my best friends. Have never done it again.

The responses were pretty much divided among the participants. When I think of seeing a club fly into the air, it does seem a bit juvenile. More importantly, it is not helping your game and is usually a sign that the game is causing you stress, not reducing it. Not to mention that we all know it is poor sportsmanship. It would certainly not be the behavior you would want your child to see or copy.

So why do some golfers throw their clubs and get angry? I spoke to several golf pros and avid golfers, and one of the most common responses was that golfers get angry because their expectation of how they think they should be playing is greater than their skill level. In other words, they think they are better than they really are.

However, you can learn to play golf to lower your stress and anxiety. The best players on tour get frustrated, but they learn to let go of the memory of that last shot and move forward with confidence and optimism. Learning to stay cool and calm under pressure becomes an art.

Now, ladies, I have to say that I have never heard of a woman throwing her club. That doesn't mean it hasn't happened – I just haven't heard of it. However, it could mean that they have a better handle on their emotions during the game.

Having taught stress management during my training career, one principle applies very clearly here: How you respond to a situation controls the outcome. Almost fifteen years ago, I attended a seminar by Jack Canfield, founder of the Chicken Soup for the Soul series of books. I learned a concept that Jack described as E + R = O. This stands for Event + Response = Outcome. We all have a choice as to how we respond, either negatively or positively. This applies to how we act on the golf course as well. Those responses will affect our outcomes. As Phil Mickelson says, "The object of golf is not just to win. It is to play like a gentleman and win."

Be Careful of the Company You Keep

Remember my dad, Jimmy, who was a caddie in the 1940s? He reminded me recently of the story of how he got fired as a young boy. He was sitting in the caddie shack waiting to be called. Suddenly, over the PA system, they called his friend Bob to come to the front office. Jimmy told his friend he would go with him to the office. They both walked into the manager's office. The manager told Bob that they had reports that he was cussing on the course and that he was fired. Then he looked at Jimmy and said, "You're fired too." Jimmy said, "Why am I fired? What did I do?" The manager replied, "If you're hanging around this bum, you're no good either." Ahhh, another lesson learned. Be careful of the company you keep on or off the course.

Will I Live Longer If I Play Golf?

You are probably thinking, "Now that's taking it a bit too far." Is it? A study published in the *Scandinavian Journal of Medicine & Science in Sports* based on data from 300,000 Swedish golfers found that golf has beneficial health effects. The Swedish Golf Federation has more than 600,000 members, out of population of 9 million people. The study found that the death rate among golfers is 40 percent lower than the rest of the population. For Swedes, this equates to an increased life expectancy of five years. An even lower death rate percentage than the average was clustered among the low-handicap golfers. In the study, golfers had a lower death rate regardless of sex, age, or social group.

Professor Anders Ahlbom, who led the study with Bahman Farahmand, said, "People play golf into old age, and there are also positive social and psychological aspects to the game that can be of help." The study does not rule out that other factors in addition to the actual playing, such as a generally healthy lifestyle, are also behind the lower death rate observed among the golfers.

I had the opportunity to talk to Professor Ahlbom. When I was talking to him about women golfers saying they didn't have enough time to play, he replied, "If you look at the research, they actually have more time to play." One other interesting point he brought up was about walking the course. He said, "In Sweden it is considered in bad taste to ride; most golfers walk." That perhaps could explain a lot.

Whether or not you think golf will help you live longer, it certainly can't hurt. However, I still go back to the simple concept of finding things you like to do. In this case, you can combine exercise, the outdoors, and friendships all at the same time.

As you walk down the fairway of life you must smell the roses, for you only get to play one round.

BEN HOGAN

The most rewarding things you do in life are most often the ones that look like they cannot be done.

ARNOLD PALMER

Chapter Ten

ENJOYING THE "SWEET SPOT" IN GOLF AND IN LIFE

In golf, the club's "sweet spot" marks the middle of the club face and is the ideal place to hit the ball. In life, I define the "sweet spot" as living your ideal life every day. To hit the sweet spot of your club takes practice in order to be consistent. To live and enjoy your ideal life every day also takes practice.

To me, living your ideal life means being the best person you can be on or off the golf course. In my speaking profession, we often talk about the importance of being the same person on or off the platform. Sometimes you see a speaker being motivational on the platform in front of the audience, and then the next time you see them they are yelling at someone at the front desk of the hotel about their room. Congruency and authenticity mean everything. This requires you to be true to yourself and realize that every interaction you have with someone presents you with an opportunity to be the best you can be. Your interaction with fellow golfers presents a similar opportunity.

Optimism

Today is a very interesting time to be alive. Our country is facing many economic and worldly challenges that filter back into family pressures. We have a choice as to how we handle these challenges. We can stick our head in the sand and wait until they go away or we can turn those challenges into opportunities and choose to live with optimism instead of fear. Optimism is important in both life and golf.

A good friend of mine, Dr. Terry Paulson, wrote a book called *The Optimism Advantage: 50 Simple Truths to Transform Your Attitudes and Actions into Results.* I asked Terry (who is also a golfer) to make the correlation between golf and optimism. Here's what he had to say:

"Nowhere is future-focused optimism more important than in golf. Life comes at you one day at a time. Golf comes at you one shot, one hole at a time. You have to learn from and then let go of the past. The focus has to be on that next shot. After all, life is like a moving vehicle with no brakes. There are no available off-ramps. There's no reverse, and you can't turn it off. That's why your rearview mirror is smaller than your front window. So don't live your life trapped in the rearview mirror! Learn what you can from the past but concentrate on what you can do now to shape your future. That will improve your golf game and your life."

After losing my mother to cancer a few years ago, I was reminded of just how precious life is. When my mother passed away suddenly from complications from her treatment, I had a difficult time accepting it. I yearned for the opportunity to talk to her again. I felt that there was still more I wanted to say to her. It just didn't seem fair, and my optimistic viewpoint was nowhere in sight.

Then, as I was going through some of her things, I came across her day-timer/address book. In the back of the book she had written these words, just as you see them below:

Life is not always fair and you better get used to it. **Be** *the best* **you** *can be.*

BARBARA WALKER

It seems that if we look close enough we can find optimism through life's experiences. Being the best you can be can take on many meanings. So often we look to others for inspiration, as opposed to looking inside ourselves to be our best self. This happens when youth look up to sports figures or celebrities and aspire to be like them. My hope is that they aspire to be themselves and be their own hero.

Challenging times will come and go, but life comes around just once. My hope for you is that you don't miss any opportunities to enjoy the "sweet spot" in golf and in life.

Warmth, kindness, and friendship are the most yearned-for commodities in the world. The person who can provide them will never be lonely.

ANN LANDERS

Chapter Eleven

ON-PAR RELATIONSHIPS

Golf is a game that is played in relationship with others. Whether enjoyed socially or for business, golf provides ample opportunities to interact and connect.

Business Relationships

Much has been written about golf as a tool for business. For years, men have made golf deals on the golf course. Women too are looking to golf to build relationships with clients. The reason this has been successful is in part because you get to spend a significant amount of time with your client in a setting outside the office. It is easier to open up and get to know the other person, which is a key step in building the relationship. Once the relationship is intact and trust is built, it opens the door for further business discussions that might not have otherwise occurred.

In order to build relationships through golf, it is critical to establish your goal. For example, is your goal to meet new potential clients, deepen existing relationships, or meet new golfers to play with? Next, consider how you will use golf to connect with others. Even if you don't golf, you could invite a client to join you as a spectator at a professional tournament. You might sponsor a hole at a golf tournament or even volunteer to work the tournament. This gives you an opportunity to meet a lot of people with similar interests.

Remember to take the time necessary to build relationships, find common ground, be a good listener, and find creative ways to stay in touch.

Improving Relationships with Your Spouse or Significant Other

My survey showed that men could actually relate golf to life lessons for relationships. One of the comments that stood out in my mind focused on the words *patience* and *respect*. Nothing is ever perfect, and any relationship takes work. One man I personally interviewed confided in me that he worked on improving his golf game harder than he worked on making his marriage work. It takes patience to master and improve your golf game. It really isn't any surprise that it also takes patience and practice to improve your relationships. As far as respect goes, that is at the top of my list. Along with respect comes trust and the desire to make the other person happy.

We talked earlier about having realistic expectations for your golf game. It makes sense that we also have realistic expectations for our relationship. Having unrealistic expectations can put added stress on the relationship.

Your attitude toward your relationship goes a long way. Every now and then, you are bound to get a bad break or get into the rough (pardon the golf pun). Maintaining a positive attitude, while not always easy, makes a huge difference. You can practice that positive attitude on the golf course too. The next time you miss a critical putt, relax instead of reacting. Set your mind on learning from that experience, and then move with a positive mindset on to the next hole.

Gay Hendrick says in his book *Conscious Golf,* "Every shot we hit goes exactly where it is supposed to go, given how it is hit. Whether our shots are 'bad' or 'good' is merely a made-up concept we've invented to keep from having fun all the time. If we are sufficiently open to learning, we can learn from every shot, every moment of life."

Communication

Communication is at the forefront of every successful business or personal relationship. Keeping the communication open and clear plays a key role. Misunderstandings can easily be blown out of proportion and cause unnecessary stress on the marriage or relationship. For example, my friend Cindy told me the story of how one of her friends first discovered the 19th hole. To protect the innocent or guilty, depending on how you look at it, the names have been changed.

Mark went golfing with his buddies. He called home to his wife Mary to tell her he was on the 19th hole. Mary said, "Okay, dinner will be ready soon." Mark hung up and went back to the 19th hole. Mary waited and another hour or two went by and it began to get dark. She couldn't understand what was taking him so long since he was just finishing the last hole when he called.

Mary called her friend Cindy to vent about Mark being late. Cindy began to laugh, and she said, "Mary, don't you know what the 19th hole is?" Mary replied, "What do you mean? It's the last hole of the game, right?" Cindy explained to Mary that there was no "real" 19th hole; there are only 18 holes, and the 19th hole is the term used to describe the pub, bar, or restaurant at the clubhouse where golfers go to have a drink and dissect the game. At this point, Mary realized there was a very big communication gap between what her husband said and what she heard. Mary went out on the front porch to wait for her husband to return. Let's just say, it wasn't a pretty sight when he returned.

The moral of the story for me is that this could all have been avoided if Mark was more up front about the 19th hole, and if Mary had a better understanding of the game. This would have opened up the conversation for a more honest dialogue. The expectations and outcome would have probably been very different.

Making sure your relationship stays on course requires continual work and nurturing on many levels. Men often joke about their "honey-do" lists. One man commented on the survey that he played golf on Saturday to get out of doing his honey-dos. Let's take a look at some honey-dos and honey-don'ts that can help your relationship.

HONEY-DOS AND HONEY-DON'TS

Honey-Dos

- Do be respectful of your spouse.
- Do tell the truth.
- Do continue to be supportive of your partner's love of the game.
- Do let your partner have their male or female bonding time.
- Do take time to play together and enjoy the sport.
- Do try to be open to doing something new and break out of the "same old, same old."
- Do keep the paths of communication open.
- Do have fun.

Honey-Don'ts

- Don't tell your partner when to play golf.
- Don't offer unsolicited golf advice.
- Don't put golf before your family and loved ones.
- Don't forget to call if you are running late.
- Don't get lost on the 19th hole.
- Don't forget to say "I love you!"

Keep your sense of humor. There's enough stress in the rest of your life not to let bad shots ruin a game you're supposed to enjoy.

AMY ALCOTT

Chapter Twelve

HOW TO HAVE FUN
REGARDLESS OF YOUR SCORE

It is very important to learn how to have fun regardless of your score. After much research, it did seem to me that men were extremely competitive on the golf course. According to a colleague and gender communication expert, Jane Sanders, competitiveness is a strong characteristic of the male gender.

A friend of mine, Jan, recently retired from nursing and has enjoyed playing the game of golf since the early 1990s. She said that she plays golf because she likes the outdoors and the challenge of competing with herself. While she was working, she and her husband played golf almost every weekend. They had a boat in the Delta and found that they were going to the boat for the weekend *just* to play golf! She said, "We never took it seriously; we wanted to enjoy the opportunity to be outside and meet other people. My husband never corrected me when we were golfing, but we played with people that we didn't know and more often than not, the male consistently corrected the female's game. It drove me nuts! Some of the men were nice and a little more quiet about the correction but others were rude and crude."

Jan also told me about another woman that stopped golfing when she was young because the males in her family were too serious about the game and would react to bad shots by throwing clubs, cursing, etc. This woman is sixty years old now and playing again and enjoying it because she doesn't take it too seriously.

It once again seems that men and women look at the game differently. If you are competing as a pro, obviously you take the game seriously, but that doesn't mean you can't have fun. And for the rest of us who aren't pros, having fun should be the priority. Whether you are looking for women's golf groups, couples golf, or seniors golf there is something for everyone.

One Man's Competitive Drive

My dad, who has been golfing for about sixty-five years, describes below one of his personal experiences on the golf course.

"I arrived at the golf course, and the person I was going to play is someone I have never beaten, which tears at my gut. I know I am a better golfer, but it has never happened. In the back of my mind I'm going to show Bob how to play this game today. We both played the first 9 even par. The second 9 Bob had a one shot lead going into the 18th tee. But Bob's tee shot went into the water, so after taking a penalty he reached the green side bunker in 3. I was now on the green in regulation 2. Bob pitched onto the green and putted in for a 5. Next, I 2 putted for a par and won by one stroke. We were both very focused on the game. Whatever was going on in our personal life at that time didn't matter for four hours that day. If a golfer is saying he plays for exercise, I don't believe it. I take that back – if he is over seventy years old, that could be the case; otherwise he is playing to beat his opponent. No one wants to lose a four-hour battle in ninety-degree heat. Sometimes we would play for a quarter a hole, or maybe a dollar on a rare occasion, and then it really gets exciting."

I asked him, "With all that competition, was it fun?" He replied, "Absolutely – I loved it! I like competing, but to me that's fun."

So you can see that people have their own interpretation about what "fun" is. However, experts tell us that the only person you should be trying to win against is yourself. That is the person who will be the hardest to beat.

A golf pro once told me something that stayed with me. He said, "Make it your intention to have fun when you play, and you'll take the edge off of your game."

Regardless of whether you play golf with men or women or a mixed group, you want to be comfortable, and it should be fun above all else! If you are feeling uncomfortable with your foursome, it is likely to increase your stress rather than reduce it. Find a good group of people that you are comfortable playing with.

WHAT MEN AND WOMEN DO DIFFERENTLY ON THE GOLF COURSE

- Women rarely if ever throw their clubs.

- Women rarely cuss on the golf course.

- Women drive the golf cart differently (or so my husband says).

- Men are more likely to play for "skins" (cash).

- Men will recap the game hole by hole when they are done.

- Men never ask if their butt looks big in their new golf pants.

Men and women are different. So what's new? Recognizing and embracing our differences can lead to great relationships and more FUN!

If you Google the word golf, you will find over 29 million links, one for almost every golfer in the U.S. Many sites will be on products, golf tips, instruction, or commentary. I found hardly anything on the Web about how to have more fun on the golf course.

TIPS FOR HAVING FUN ON THE GOLF COURSE

1. Don't take yourself so seriously.

2. Set realistic expectations.

3. Don't focus on the score.

4. Learn the fundamentals.

5. Allow time to socialize after the game.

6. Connect and get to know the other players.

7. Set your intention on having fun – and relax!

Listen to the Beat

Music can be incredibly motivating and is known for setting the mood for any number of activities. For example, can you imagine a baseball game, a wedding, a pep rally, or a movie without music? Imagine the movie *Jaws* without that famous music playing right when you know the shark is going to appear. Without a doubt, music sets the mood and tone. It can also add an element of fun to your practice time at the driving range.

In my research, I discovered a company called Tempo in Motion. It was founded by Mike Boyko, an entrepreneur that combined his love of golf with his passion for music to create a unique product. He was a rock-and-roll drummer for most of his life. Mike developed a sports training aid to improve a golfer's swing. The music is a way to motivate and focus while being "in the zone." The click track is a motion sequence that guides your movement throughout the music track with the purpose of building muscle memory and a consistent rhythm. The combination of the click track and the music helps you to groove your golf swing and ultimately swing through with more power and more distance. On his website (www.tempoinmotion.com), you can find the tempo that addresses your swing pattern.

No matter what musical style fits you (metal, rock, ambient, jazz, crossover, or country), Tempo in Motion has a track for you and your swing. This is a downloadable track that you can download to your iPod, MP3 player, or cell phone. You can then take that to the driving range and use it to practice your swing. Music can bring more fun and mood elevation to your practice time.

I have not yet had the opportunity to try this, but I'm open to the idea and it sounds like a unique way to help your golf game and have fun at the same time. The key here is to find what works for you to make the game more enjoyable and, above all else, more fun.

PUT ON A HAPPY FACE

I heard a story recently about a man who used to get extremely frustrated on the golf course when he didn't get the score he'd hoped for. To rid himself of his attachment to his score, he developed a unique system. At the end of each hole, if he felt he'd had more good shots than bad, he would draw a happy face on the scorecard next to that hole. If he had more bad shots, he would draw a sad face. At the end of the day, if he had more happy faces, he considered it to be a good day. That worked for him. If you don't put too much pressure on yourself, you are more likely to have a happy face day. Sounds good to me!

*The most important thing in communication
is to hear what isn't being said.*

PETER DRUCKER

Chapter Thirteen

HOW TO KEEP TEEING IT UP

In order to keep teeing it up, the answer is quite simple. Above all, it is important to be open and honest with your spouse or significant other. Respect each other and create opportunities for quality time together on and off the golf course. In many cases, this may mean compromise or creatively finding the win-win. Life is short, and the value of making your significant other feel important goes a long way. This might mean a kind word or action, or it might simply mean being supportive of activities that the other person enjoys.

Golf, like relationships, requires practicing good habits that make each day better than the last. To get better and have fun in golf, you have to keep teeing it up. By making your relationship the priority, you just might find that you improve your score on and off the course. Enjoy the journey!

Don't forget to visit our website, www.HoneyILoveGolf. com, to learn more and take advantage of special offers.

TIPS TO KEEP TEEING IT UP

1. Make your relationship the priority.

2. Make time for each other.

3. Show your appreciation and respect daily.

4. Respect each other's differences.

5. Communicate effectively and often.

6. Schedule time for golf with your friends. (Check the family calendar first.)

7. Schedule time for golf with your spouse or loved one.

8. Celebrate and enjoy the golf lifestyle.

9. Tell your partner the things you love about them.

10. Remind your partner: Honey, I Love Golf, but I Love You More!

PART FIVE

ACTION PLAN

PUT YOUR PLAN INTO ACTION

Goals for Golf

_____

_____

_____

_____

_____

_____

_____

Goals to Improve My Relationship

_____

_____

_____

_____

_____

_____

_____

PUT YOUR PLAN INTO ACTION

Golf Lifestyle and Vacation Goals

_____

_____

_____

_____

_____

_____

_____

Life, love, relationships, and yes, GOLF! Who would have thought it? I think the message is simple. We can learn from any experience. The challenge is to apply what we learn, whether it is in golf or in life. Remember, life is worth loving – don't forget to tell someone today that you love them, and put your goals into action!

ABOUT THE AUTHOR

JODI WALKER is a professional speaker, author, and consultant. She is the founder and president of Success Alliances, a training and development company. Jodi has earned the prestigious Certified Speaking Professional designation, given to fewer than 7 percent of the speakers from the International Federation of Speakers and the National Speakers Association.

Jodi helps organizations improve communication, reduce stress, enhance creativity, build leaders at all levels, and develop their "entrepreneurial thinking® skills." Her mantra is Helping Organizations Move Beyond Business and Life as Usual.

After growing up with a family of golfers and then marrying one, Jodi found herself struggling to understand why her husband loved the game of golf so much. Her research and personal experiences paved the way for *Honey, I Love Golf, But I Love You More!* It is her desire to help women understand why their men love golf so passionately and to help both men and women use that knowledge to improve their relationship. In addition, Jodi loves sharing with women how they too can benefit from the "golf lifestyle."

Jodi is available to speak at business, golf, or charity events. For more information, visit her websites:

www.HoneyILoveGolf.com

www.JodiWalker.com

Breinigsville, PA USA
28 October 2010
248187BV00004B/1/P